THE
WAIKATO

Green Heartland of New Zealand

Photography by Graeme Matthews
Text by James Ritchie

THE
WAIKATO

Green Heartland of New Zealand

Photography by Graeme Matthews
Text by James Ritchie

Published by
Graeme Matthews
PHOTO IMAGE
193 Rarangi Beach Road
Blenheim, New Zealand
Phone/Fax (03) 570 5655

Edited by Christine Cole Catley, Picton
Map Illustration by Kelvin Allen
Typography by Carmen Thayer

Thanks to the following people who have helped with this project:
Craig Nicholson, James & Jane Ritchie, Arthur Beale, Cushla Denton,
Turangawaewae Marae, Barry Brailsford, David & Karen Walmsley,
Barry Sullivan, Richard Wallace, Robert Hewitt, Sammy Thomson,
Waitomo Caves, Robert Tahi, Judi Beaton, David Thorp, Hank Snow,
Netherton Primary School, Majella Heaton, Kelvin Allen, Jim &
Diana Webber, Carmen Thayer, Chris Catley, Coral Orsman, and
most of all my wife Jenny; and all those people who have helped in
some way.

Photographs copyright © 1998 Graeme Matthews
Essay copyright © 1998 James Ritchie

Published 1998
Printed in Hong Kong

Paperback ISBN 0-473-04705-5
Hardback ISBN 0-473-04704-7

THE
WAIKATO

Waikato River ○ Port Waika

Ra

Brida
Fa

Kaw

0   10   2
Scale 1:5

Waikato te awa
Taupiri te maunga
Potatau te tangata

The Land, The Waters, The People; the sacred icons of Waikato Maori come together as the river enters its lower gorge. It is guarded here by Taupiri where rest the graves of generations of Tainui ancestors and all of the Kings.

Beginnings

Some 230 million years ago, the great southern continent, Gondwanaland, began to break up. That part of it which ultimately became New Zealand was pushed against and under the Australian plate by irresistible and intensely powerful forces. From the grinding collision arose the mountains and volcanoes which built New Zealand.

The Waikato territory rests upon the original founding plate, limestone and greywacke laid down by ancient oceans. These base materials are now overlaid and deeply enriched by the erosion debris of those mountains and by repeated volcanic ash showers.

These lands are watered by the longest river in the land, rising on the high slopes of volcanic Tongariro to reach Lake Taupo and then to the Tasman Sea; in all, some 500 kilometres from the mountain to the coast. Over millennia, repeatedly, white-hot flows of gases and pumice of immense proportions poured out of the caldera that now form the lakes at Rotorua and Taupo, burying the land in deep deposits. These clogged the river and forced it to find a new outfall to the sea. This has happened many, many times, the last perhaps as recently as a thousand years ago.

Between each of these dramatic events, the river slowly built the deep loam soils of its basin and surrounding valleys. Like sentinels around these flatlands stand the extinct cones of numerous volcanoes, quiet now, as they have been for at least the last million years.

Upon these lands, mountain and plain, arose the original primordial forests. Some retain the plants and trees carried from Gondwanaland but volcanic destruction modified the forests, creating isolated and distinct ecosystems. All these forests flourished and evolved, slowly changing, relatively untouched until the first human contact brought fire. The Waikato then passed through another transformation into unforested sweeping tussock and scrub lands with islands of the old-growth timber trees here and there. Around the edges of the basin the eroded, bush-clad volcanic peaks of previous eruptions remained, as did also the limestone outcrops of the original basic plate.

The first humans, Maori, came probably about 350 a.d., certainly by 650, and in the mythical traditional migration of canoes in 1350. One of the canoes, the Tainui, it is told made its journey from Rarotonga to make its landfall, caught in the hook of the Bay of Plenty. From there it journeyed to where Auckland is now, was carried across the isthmus to the Tasman Sea, finally sailing on to explore and find its resting place on the west coast. There it remains just inside the entrance to the drowned harbour at Kawhia. The people placed it on a raised hillock, an ahurewa, an altar dedicated to the atua, the gods, and great stones still mark where it lies behind the historic meeting house a Maketu.

From there the Tainui people spread up and down the coast and over the hills to occupy the two great river systems of the region, the Waikato and the Waipa. Their fires cleared the central valleys as they developed their lifestyle, first as hunters and gatherers, dependent on shore, lake, river and forest foods, and later as intensive agriculturalists. There they lived in clans of one or two hundred mostly at bends in the rivers where a trench thrown across a loop provided safety from attack and ready access to the river as a highway. The population grew to around 25,000 by the time the first European discoverers arrived.

These were rich lands which they defended fiercely and gradually learned how to nurture and to understand. The river was their major highway, rich in legend and folklore, revered as an ancestor. Its name became their name and is so still. Hills and mountains were often named for places in the ancient Polynesian homeland, Hawaiki. Others came to carry personal ancestral names or were named for battles or other events. But the river was the most honoured feature for it linked them all in history and in daily living.

In 1769 James Cook rediscovered the land and recognised that the people of Tainui were numerous. What he did not know was that they were gradually expanding their boundaries, colonising the hinterland still, and were soon to unite into a large federation emerging as the dominant tribal power of the northern island.

Drifting immigrants, European traders and others, began to settle, first at the mouth then up the river, around all of the harbours of the west coast, spilling over to outposts in the interior. Missionaries of various faiths travelled the old Maori trails, noting the landforms, the villages and sometimes the beliefs and traditions of the people. The Tainui people incorporated these newcomers, married them in, and took over their new means of production, of literacy, of communication, to develop a new political economy of which Tainui themselves were the owners and controllers. They ran schooners around the coast, across the Tasman even, for they had always been traders.

To protect their lands and maintain their authority and power, the Tainui people recognised the need for unity. By the 1820s they had federated for purely internal reasons. As a whole tribe they did not sign the Treaty at Waitangi in 1840 but remained aloof under their own leadership – their Arikinui. Later they held discussions with the other major tribes and in 1856 agreed to set up a king to govern them, Te Wherowhero, who then took the name of King Potatau. His descendant, Te Arikinui Dame Te Atairangikaahu, who has her headquarters in Ngaruawahia, the historic centre of Waikato, is the sixth in direct line to hold the office.

After the Treaty, foreign settlers began to come to New Zealand in increasing waves. They, especially the rising merchants of Auckland, turned envious eyes upon the rich flat lands of the Waikato. They wished to control the produce coming from them and sought to destroy the central power of the Maori King. Thus in 1863 false charges of rebellious intent were fabricated by the government. The Waikato was invaded. Waikato Tainui were forced from their homelands.

Devastated at the suddenness, injustice and betrayal of this action, and by the overthrow of their dominion over their own lands, the Waikato Maori withdrew to the southern hills. There, in what came to be called the King Country, they lived with their kinsfolk for 25 years.

The government confiscated 1.5 million acres of their land. From this loss they would never recover. This colonial government folly plunged the Waikato Maori into tragedy from which they suffered for more than a century thereafter.

The Waikato Grows

Three times in its history the Waikato has flourished and fulfilled the promise of its richness. The first was in the millennia before people ever came when the climate and soil produced a temperate rainforest of prolific diversity. Then the pre-contact Maori became skilled horticulturalists as well as utilising the original foods of fish, fowl and forest; an economy which amply supported their needs. After white settlers came, the development of the Waikato staggered, suffering a series of setbacks until well into this century. These disrupted progress in the region until, at last, prosperity returned.

Even the sporadic bursts of wealth that gold booms or wool sales occasionally provided for the colony as a whole did little for the Waikato. It was not until farming became a science and an industry, after World War II, that the region began to fulfil its potential. Even now its export-based agricultural economy is vulnerable to market and financial fluctuations.

After the war of the 1860s the confiscated land was surveyed and lots were offered to the troops and mercenaries who had fought for the government. Very few of them stayed to settle. Most readily sold their interests if buyers could be found. The rest of the confiscated lands were to be sold to finance the building of roads and railways, to establish rural townships and implant some sort of orderly governance, but again ready buyers were few. The region remained empty of people and production for decades after the Land Wars.

The colony as a whole was struggling and little capital arose from the exploitation of its original resources, flax, timber, gold and whale oil.

Socially the Waikato had become a lawless wasteland. Tribal control had been broken and no other established. The region became an uneasy hinterland; its richness lay fallow.

In these days the new town of Hamilton (carrying the name of an obscure colonel and founded on town land grants to the colonial troops) stumbled slowly into life. Standing astride the river, with a military road to Auckland, another to Raglan and a third to Tauranga, it was well situated to become a hub of the Waikato as indeed, in time, it did. But it was ill drained, exposed, surrounded by swamps, cold and frequently foggy and frosty in winter.

In the wider region a few surrounding towns struggled to grow, usually around large landholdings. Thus Morrinsville, Cambridge, Oxford (which later reverted, unpretentiously, to its original name, Tirau) and Huntly began. Others simply grew from Maori settlements, occupied or abandoned, such as Pirongia, Te Awamutu, Te Kuiti, Otorohanga, Matamata, Raglan, Port Waikato and Kawhia. It was not till 1877 that the tiny centre, Hamilton (population then 1243!) became a borough. The Maori population in the region was eight times this.

That year the rail-line to Auckland came through but even that made little difference. Hamilton may have become the hub, but of what? Just a centre of rural poverty. It needed people and capital to grow but the Waikato had neither. The Coromandel gold strikes fed the growth of Auckland directly; Waikato drifted back into the mists of the river and the fogs of the swamp.

What was worse, much of the land was mysteriously sick. The European grasses grew but cattle could not thrive on them. Something was wrong. It was not until the 1920s that the secret was found; volcanic ash showers had left some Waikato soils lacking trace elements essential for healthy growth. Scientific soil testing and the addition of appropriate minerals to annual applications of superphosphate and lime were the solution and suddenly opened the area. But then came two world wars, The Great Depression between them, and it was only then that the key turned to open the treasure-house of the Waikato. Banks and bankers, once referred to as the misery of miners and the miners of misery, began to invest in the development of farming. Government research into agriculture, stock improvement, horticulture, soils and grasslands became established at various stations in the Waikato. At last the land began to flower again. Now a million people live in the wider region. It has become the churning factory of the dairy industry, a forest production centre, a powerhouse of energy production and, for all the development, a charming and beautiful place to live.

In 1881 the Maori King returned to live again in his home region. Peace was declared but without recompense. Reconstruction of the tribe and its identity was slow particularly as repeated epidemics were decimating the Maori population. The people returned with him and settled in small pockets of reserve land or with relatives whose land had not been taken because they had supported the colonial army, kinship overcoming disloyalty to the Maori King and the tribal federation he represented.

After the turn of the century a powerful woman, Te Puea Herangi, cousin to the King, took control of tribal development.

She personally raised a family of around 40 orphaned children and with them rebuilt a community at Ngaruawahia. This became first a headquarters for the tribe, and then a national marae where the influence of the King could again be seen and felt in the land. World War II disrupted her plans but by mid-century Tainui had re-emerged as a major tribe and began to search for redress for the iniquities they had suffered. Now numbering more than 35,000 people, Waikato have re-established their presence and their mana. In 1947 Te Puea facilitated the establishment of the Tainui Maori Trust Board which eventually negotiated settlement in 1995 for the confiscated lands.

Other features contributed to the growth of the Waikato: energy, forestry and bloodstock farming. That there was coal in the lower river basin had been known to Maori and Pakeha alike from early times. War brought the first paddle steamer to the Waikato in 1863 but steamers had been active well before that. After the war the gunboats became riverboats on the great waterway of the Waikato. Most burned wood but gradually coal took over after 1876 when commercial mining really began. When the railway went through, the mining of coal greatly expanded, especially as the destruction of the original forests reduced the supply of wood as fuel.

Then in 1913 the first hydro-electric station on the river was built, followed in the 1940s by the construction of many more. The necessary roads and service centres added general infrastructure, opening more of the area for development. Since then geothermal and thermal generation have expanded this aspect of the Waikato economy. Exotic forestry came late in the day after it was found that an obscure Californian conifer, pinus radiata, grew to maturity here with almost incredible rapidity and on land that was otherwise of little use. Prison and relief labour by unemployed men during the Great Depression in the 1930s expanded the planting. But it was not till the 1950s that industrial development began to harvest the tree crop in any quantity. The availability of the waters of the Waikato was a salient factor in deciding location, and townships grew rapidly around the major sites.

The entry of bloodstock and stud breeding was also a post-war development, though earlier beginnings had shown the way. Every little town had its racecourse, and the calendar of race meetings established a social round that linked the region as much as any other interest. The racing and breeding industries developed as natural partners.

So, finally, wealth came to the Waikato, nationally vital and in export terms mighty. Little boroughs grew up around the little towns; little towns along the railway line, then the main highway as well as on the river. Many were squat and ugly but not in the eyes of their citizens. They built their local halls, for meetings and dances and the inevitable marriages and twenty-first birthday parties. They also built their little churches and the odd museum. More wars added more memorials, little riverside parks and walkways. Topdressing intensified the greenness as well as the wealth. The Waikato had come of age.

The Waikato Now

From where it rises on the upper icy slopes of volcanic Ruapehu, to the shingle flats and holiday shacks of its mouth, the 500 kilometres of the Waikato river tell its own story. Virtually every metre of its fall is now tamed by eight hydro dams that produce 1050 megawatts of power. Add two geothermal stations and the massive 1000 megawatt coal and gas fired thermal station at Huntly and you are looking at a quarter of New Zealand's electric supply.

When, in the 1970s, the Tongariro power scheme captured much of the melt water from the snow fields of Ruapehu, the extra flow down the Waikato required extensive stopbanking to provide downstream protection. So the entire river system is now controlled. At set times water may be released, to control flooding or simply to allow recreational white-water rafting, but to the eye of the beholder the river is now a sleeping taniwha, a placid water spirit.

A further contribution to the nation's energy needs comes from the vast sub-bituminous coal deposits of the Waikato field. The resource of some two billion tonnes is barely touched by the current annual extraction of 1.5 millon tonnes. This is 43 percent of the national output, much of it used now in steel production.

If you gaze out from any one of the old weathered volcanic peaks that define the edges of the Waikato basin your eye sweeps over lands that yield nearly half the dairying production in the country, a good part of its cropping and orcharding land, most of its prestigious stud breeding industry, and substantial forestry. Whatever its past, the region looks fat and healthy now; the green grass grows year round.

Dairy herds average 200 cows in a single unit – the largest milking as many as 950 twice a day; that's a lot of beef, milk and butter. Between 1965 and 1985 production doubled simply through better grassland management and herd improvement. As export prices rise and fall so too does the wealth of the Waikato, but underneath lie those deep loamy soils, and earthy security. But there is more to the region than hoof and horn. Around each of the little towns of the Waikato there is a flourishing industrial fringe, often there to service rural needs but now diversified into furniture making, tourism, wineries, small manufacturing, electronics, fishing, aeronautic servicing and aerial top-dressing, farm and motor machinery, as well as all the services a modern region needs.

Each little town has its cultural life too, and even nightlife if you look for it. Many have their own small museums, arts and craft centres, spinning, weaving and embroidery groups and music-makers. Remember Split Enz? The brothers Finn come from Te Awamutu. Dame Kiri te Kanawa was born close by. Gardens? Roses? Some of the best.

Auckland, big, rough and rude, is just a car ride away, a great place to go shopping but who wants to live there when you can visit when you want? In contrast, Waikato people will tell you that they have outgrown their subservience to their Big Neighbour; they have values the city can never emulate, quietness, beauty, tranquillity, and the best ice cream and milk shakes (and dairy factories) in the world. Hamilton, once a cow-town, has just become our town, a city self-sufficient but by no means smug.

Waikato is also a playground that few outsiders know about. There are tramping routes in all the surrounding hills in marvellous temperate rainforest. The coastline has the phenomenal Raglan surf-breaks, a full kilometre ride when the waves are right and world-famous for its left point breaks. The coasts are playgrounds and the ski fields a few hours' drive away. The trout fishing too is a secret to be shared.

The Waitomo area is well known for its glow-worm caves. Now there is also black-water rafting, riding tubes through underground streams, abseiling, kayaking, hunting, and mountain biking and there is white-water rafting on many streams and rivers, and general caving for the adventurous. The racing calendar is full as befits an area where superior studs are everywhere. There is also rugby. Where once there was mostly production there are now pleasures as well.

The Maori presence in the region has been restored through the efforts of the people themselves. There are more than 60 marae or communal centres, many with carved meeting houses, early child care centres where the Maori language is nurtured, and usually a dining and recreational hall too. Here Maori people can continue their customary life, especially social gatherings of all kinds, where the language is heard, the ancient songs sung, dances danced, youth groups meet to enjoy themselves and there are death wakes, tangi. Some marae now have health centres where healing from both cultures can be sought and found. Maori are no longer marginal to the life of the region but participate fully in all that it offers.

The region has also become a major centre for tertiary education. Hamilton has a fine technical institute. There is a Maori equivalent, the Aotearoa Institute. The University of Waikato, just 30 years old, now has 15,000 students, an annual budget of $150 million, a close association with several top-line research institutes and a profound Maori presence. Nearly one quarter of its students are Maori and its faculties include a specialist School of Maori and Pacific Development and its associated Research Centre.

The university stands on lands owned by the tribes of Waikato, a result of the settlement reached between the Crown and Waikato to resolve the grievance created by the land confiscations in the 1860s. From this settlement the tribal corporation now holds diversified assets in fishing, forestry, farming, real estate, and tourism, is transforming two old military bases for industrial and educational uses and building a new future through educational grants and services to its marae communities. Its asset base is approaching a quarter of a billion dollars in value, built over less than a decade of operations.

The Waikato has outgrown its old reputation as a collection of backward cow-towns. Maybe it lacks the dramatic grandeur of the mountain landscapes of the southern island, and the excitement of big cities, yet it is moving and modernising; confident without complacency, Waikato people make no apology for who they are and where they live.

The Waikato now reveals the riches which were always there. There is harmony now. Its history behind it, Waikato is making its future.

James Ritchie

Tangi-te-korowhiti is the venerated Pohutukawa tree to which the Tainui canoe was tied on arrival in Kawhia harbour around 1350 AD.

Before the arrival of the Tainui people, the land around Kawhia and much of the Waikato was occupied by tribes of earlier migrations, seaward Ngati Hikawai and Te Upokotioa, inland the Kahu-punga-punga tribe. The origins of these earlier arrivals are lost in the mists of time. Tainui killed the men and married the women; a quick and efficient way to occupy a new land. By the mid-sixteenth century the Tainui had spread fron Kawhia to begin a long history of inter-tribal warfare.

From time to time the branches of Tangi-te-korowhiti fall but the tree regenerates and lives on, as do its people.

Kawhia moana
Kawhia tangata
Kawhia kai

The sea
The people
The richness

Previous pages: One canoe, one people
On a grassy slope just up from the waters edge of Kawhia Harbour stand two upright stone markers. These are said to mark the bow and stern of a buried waka, the first Tainui waka that landed here. It was buried according to Maori custom.

Photographer's note:
I found it an emotional experience to stand here on a peaceful summer evening and imagine that arrival from a foreign land and to ponder on the custom of burying their only means of transport; saying in effect, "there is no going back; here we settle and begin a new life".

The Meeting House at Kawhia, Auaukiterangi, protects the hill behind, where the canoe still lies.
So to enter this, the most central and traditional place for all of the Tainui tribes, one must pass under
a representation of the waka and its guardians.

The symbolic lifeline of the region, the Waikato River weaves its way into the region from the south. Seen here soon after leaving Lake Taupo, the river winds northward for 425 kilometres through the Waikato district before meeting the Tasman Sea.

Above: The ocean coast of the Waikato where the Tasman Sea meets the land is wild and rugged. But just south of the outlet of Raglan Harbour, shown here, it offers surfers some of the most consistent and reliable breaks in the world.

Opposite: The drowned harbour of Raglan, seen here at low tide, reaches 30 kilometres inland, with serene little bays and beaches.

Previous pages: People have probably lived on the peninsula at Raglan for over 1500 years. It was once a flourishing Maori trading centre and later a port for the west coast shipping and fishing trade. Now Raglan is a sleepy seaside resort whose people seek no glamour and whose lifestyle is an almost secret treasure.
It nestles under its sacred mountain Karioi, a name derived from a place in the mythic homeland, Hawaiki, and signifying lingering repose.

Above: The coastal farms of the western Waikato run mostly sheep. Coastal conditions and long dry summers burn off the grasses. The farms are large compared with the dairy farms on the lush green plains further inland, but conditions are harsher with drying seawinds resulting in some years seeing no rain for three-month spells.

Opposite: Local farmer Sammy Thomson. In recent and historic times the coastal Waikato Maori comprised two major tribes, Ngati Tahinga (Sammy's origins), and Ngati Mahanga. They controlled from the coast to the Waikato River, between Port Waikato and Kawhia. Though they intermarried, their tribal pride often led to conflict. Today they have many small settlements throughout the district.

Above: Few people except the locals travel the dirt road from Raglan to the little hamlet at Port Waikato. But if you take that road you may begin to appreciate how Maori and European farmers have lived together here for 150 years with little conflict and much understanding.

Opposite: Local mailman Barry Sullivan should know his way round these country roads by now; after all, he's been doing this mail run for the last 18 years.

Previous pages: The loneliness of the coastal road north of Raglan to Port Waikato. The suddenness with which one finds oneself in what seems like total remoteness is one of the great charms of this region.

Hamilton

Above: Hamilton, spanning the Waikato River, is the hub of the many prosperous farm centres that are spread throughout the region. The city grew from a small Ngati Wairere village, Kirikiriroa. As its name implied, it was just a long sandbank; a river landing site. Indeed it was not a first choice for a settler city site; Pirongia had that honour and was to be renamed Alexandra.

The Land Wars changed all that. Centrality and strategy made Hamilton the chosen site and it grew slowly from soldier settlement land grants to become New Zealand's fourth largest city.

Some wish that it had been named after Lord Nelson's beautiful mistress, but this is not so. Captain Fane Charles Hamilton, a naval person who died at the battle of Gate Pa in Tauranga in 1864, gave his name. Now it is a hub city of 120,000.

No-one has written a novel called *The Bridges of Hamilton City*, but they have their own stories. Union Bridge, built in 1879, was later called Victoria after the old Queen.

This one, Fairfield, opened the fair fields to the city's north and east for suburban development in 1937. It allowed stock from across the river to be herded right through to the railway-yards at Frankton. The railway itself had crossed the river in 1884. Other bridges followed, till there are now six, with maybe more to come.

Now the city is opening up to the river, with new vistas and walkways.

Previous pages: From the earliest days the Waikato River was a highway. Maori paddled their waka from the coast to Cambridge, and upstream of here they made portages past rapids and waterfalls all the way to Lake Taupo. They navigated the Waipa River up to Taumaranui. Later the Waikato River became a busy route for commerce and trade.

Today only the *MV Waipa Delta* remains. She provides three cruises a day along the Hamilton reaches. For all her old-world paddle steamer appearance she is only 12 years old and fitted out for pleasure rather than trade. But once the river had many like her, and even, for a short and terrible time, gun-boats to support the invading troops during the Land Wars of the 1860s.

Lake Rotoroa and the recreation reserves around it provide a buffer between Hamilton's city centre and its industrial suburb, Frankton.

You can jog, walk the dog, swim, sit, play frisbie, fly a kite, or paddle and sail on the water. But you can't launch a motorboat.

The lake itself is a bit of a mystery. It has no obvious in or outflow, yet stays healthy and well.

A great place for...

a picnic

kids

and ducks.

The Waikato River, as it flows through the city, is a great facility for water recreation such as canoeing and rowing training. In addition to this it can also be enjoyed from the riverbank walkway which takes three hours to walk, taking the circuit along one bank and returning along the other.

Previous pages: The Waikato climate, temperate and moist, will grow almost anything, from anywhere, which is one reason why Hamilton is so green and well-treed.
Its residents garden, almost fanatically, and enjoy planting along the river and in the parklands that began with its founders. But also the early influence of Ruakura, when it was a government horticultural research centre, gave Hamilton gardens variety and interest.

Tales (tails) of the riverbank.
Dogs think that the walks alongside the Waikato River were made for them.

Photographer's note:
I was on the lookout for a photo along the riverbank which is such a wonderful part of Hamilton. Along came a jogger with his dog and I thought it might enliven the scene to include the dog. I was surprised when the dog stood still for me and the owner said he liked posing for the camera. I swear the dog is smiling in the shot.

Music at the open-air
market held in Frankton
every Saturday morning.

Photographer's note:
*I was parked in Victoria Street and
had noticed this concrete-like statue
on the footpath. It was a real surprise
when this slightly built lady came out
from the adjacent shop and picked it
up under one arm and carried it
inside.*

Garden Place, Hamilton.

Founded in 1964, the Waikato University has grown rapidly into a $150 million per year enterprise. It rightly lays claim to modernity and an innovative style. One-quarter of its students are Maori, and Tainui owns the campus site which is leased to the university; a unique arrangement from which both benefit.

Next Pages: Farmland near Te Awamutu, in the late afternoon. A blend of green pasture, hedgerows and trees.

Waitomo Caves

Above: To experience the underground world of the Waitomo Caves in the King Country is overwhelming.

The glow-worm grotto contains thousands of glow-worm larvae all sending their luminous glow from the cave roof, as an attempt to attract insects which are then snared on hanging filaments covered with sticky beads.

Visitors glide silently underneath this magical canopy of 'stars' in a motorless boat, pulled along by the guide using unseen ropes in the darkness. The effect is breathtaking.

Opposite: Aranui Cave, some 2 kilometres beyond the glow-worm cave, shows how thousands of years of dripping water have sculpted glorious patterns and colours in the limestone.

This interesting cave was discovered in 1910 by a Maori hunter, Te Rutuku Aranui,whose dog had chased a pig through the hidden cave entrance.

Above: Maori mark any place of significance with a pou whenua, a
land post. This one, outside the Waitomo glow-worm caves, may
seem just a marker for tourists but it is more than that. It is a
guardian for the mana of the land and the caves.
The glow-worms need all the protection they can get as their ecology
is delicate and fragile.

Opposite: Bridal Veil Falls, between Raglan and Kawhia. It needs a short walk from the road to see
this spectacular waterfall. A viewing platform alongside the top of the falls gives a giddy view of its
55-metre plunge, while another at the pool edge below gives the view shown here.

Distinctive Buildings

Waipa Tavern, Ngaruawahia.

Most towns still have a traditional old pub, one that has somehow managed to survive the fires that have consumed so many of these old wooden buildings.
The bright red building in Te Aroha is now a cafe but was formerly an important bank in the town; surely a bank which is now in the red.

Rangiriri Tavern, Rangiriri

Post Office, Paeroa. Built 1926.

Cafe, Te Aroha. Built 1923.

Paeroa Hotel, Paeroa. Shifted here 1904.

Delta Tavern, Ngaruawahia.

Nottingham Castle Hotel, built 1914.

The lush pastures of the Waikato have raised many thoroughbred racehorses to race on the racetracks of the world.
Cambridge Stud, shown here, was the home of the legendary sire, Sir Tristram.

Photographer's note:
I became aware of just how far the fame of this area has reached when I was driving through Sweden. When the person working at the petrol station saw New Zealand on my credit card, his face lit up as he said, "Ah, Sir Tristram."

Cambridge

Above: Trees, through all the seasons of the year, are the special feature of this town, making it one of New Zealand's most attractive.

Cambridge began as a military camp in 1864, with soldiers pitching their tents along the terraces on both sides of the Waikato River. Earlier it was an important Maori settlement, called Horotiu.

The first missionary to pass through here wrote: "It was as though we travelled all the way from Ngarawahia to Horotiu through gardens, so intensive was the native agriculture."

Opposite: Te Koutu Lake in Cambridge is a real gem. The lake is hidden away in a tree-surrounded basin, but is well worth searching out. It has important links with Tainui Maori tradition.

After the Land Wars, Tawhiao, the second Maori King, longingly referred to it as the washbasin of his sorrows, as though to return here again might alleviate the pain of his loss.

Water contained

Water contained:

Within, by the Water Tower at Cambridge. It was built in 1903 to hold water pumped up from Moon Creek. It was closed 23 years later when the township got a better water supply elsewhere. Now the town's water comes from reservoirs near Karapiro Dam.

Without, by the Karapiro Dam (*opposite page*) at the outlet of Lake Karapiro. This is the last in the chain of eight hydro power stations on the Waikato River. After this the river is free to make its way unimpeded to the sea. The lake formed behind the dam has become New Zealand's top rowing course.

THIS TABLET
WAS ERECTED BY THE SOLDIERS of H.M. 65th Regiment
AS A MEMORIAL of The NEW ZEALANDERS WHO FELL IN THE
ACTIONS AT RANGIAOHIA ON THE 21st AND 22nd FEBRUARY 1864
AND AT ORAKAU ON THE 31st MARCH 1st AND 2nd APRIL 1864

I SAY UNTO YOU. LOVE YOUR ENEMIES.   J.R. LXV.

SUFFER THE LITTLE   LDREN

Above: In Old St. John's Church in Te Awamutu is a plaque erected during the Waikato Land Wars.
The memorial was paid for and erected by ordinary soldiers of the British Regiment based here, a
symbol of the respect which they held for their Maori opponents.
The last battle, at Orakau, was fought near here in 1863.

Previous pages: Te Awamutu. In the nineteenth century the Te Awamutu area had a large Maori
population. They built defensive pa sites in loops of rivers and on hilltops with good vantage points.
The settlement became established at the start of the Land Wars in 1863. It was known as Te Awamutu,
meaning "end of the river", and became a centre for government forces during the Land Wars.
The railway from Auckland reached here in 1880 and the settlement began to accelerate.
Today it is an important farming service township with a population of 9,000.

Monuments to a Turbulent Past

Maniapoto Monument, Kihikihi

Rangiriri

IT WAS RECORDED GOVERNOR SIR GEORGE GREY'S PROPOSAL TO WARRIOR CHIEF REWI MANIAPOTO THAT HE LIVE AT KIHIKIHI AS A GESTURE OF MAORI AND PAKEHA UNITY.
SIR GEORGE GREY SAID TO HIM AT WAITARA ON JUNE 28 1878 'REWI, LET US PLANT OUR TREE OF PEACE AT KIHIKIHI IN THE MIDST OF OUR CHILDREN AND WHEN THIS TREE BEARS FRUIT OUR CHILDREN, BOTH MAORI AND PAKEHA, CAN HELP THEMSELVES'.
THIS MONUMENT WAS ERECTED TO THE MEMORY OF -REWI MANIAPOTO- 1807, 21ST JUNE 1894.
THE LAST REMAINING ELDER CHIEF OF THE NGATI MANIAPOTO OF NGATI RAUKAWA AND A GREAT LEADER OF THE MAORI PEOPLE.
DURING HIS LIFETIME HE WAS A CUSTODIAN OF HARMONY BETWEEN EUROPEAN AND MAORI AND HELD STEADFAST TO THE PRINCIPLES OF THE SEAL OF THE TREATY OF WAITANGI.

Maniapoto Monument, Kihikihi

Near Ngaruawahia

Scattered throughout the district are reminders of the short period which began in 1863 when a greedy government set Pakeha against Maori in the Land Wars, to the desolation of both. Previous to this there had been marriages, friendships and partnerships between the cultures; many withstood the war. The governor and government of the time came to regret their actions, and eventually in 1995 Queen Elizabeth II formally apologised to Tainui for loss of life and land. A settlement was reached, and Tainui forgave their conquerors. These monuments take on a new significance now.

Orakau

Above: Pine trees lie stacked at the Kinleith mill, ready to be converted into building timber, paper, or pulp.

Opposite: Morning mists provide moisture for pine forests in the southern part of the region. Part of the central volcanic plateau, the soils here are fertile for tree-growing. Many volcanic explosions from the bowels of the earth have spread their coatings of ash and minerals over the land. The land itself, much of it out of sight of the road traveller, is dissected in many places by deep, rugged ravines.

Previous pages: Waikato the river, defines Waikato the district. Now calm and peaceful, over time its waters have pushed through to many outlets, gradually building the rich fertility of what was once its flood plain. Hydro dams now control its flow, as here at the southern end of Lake Karapiro.

Twilight sheds its last light of the day on the huge timber, pulp and paper mills at Kinleith, eight kilometres south of Tokoroa.
Operated by Carter Holt Harvey Forests Ltd, the mills are a big employer for nearby Tokoroa.

Tokoroa

Winter frost still whitens the areas of ground around Tokoroa township.
In the south of the Waikato district, Tokoroa sits on the undulating plain of the North Island's central volcanic plateau. Forty years ago there was virtually nothing here but trees.
The large timber industry that the town is based on has created a multi-cultural society here.
Population is about 17,000, of which one-third are Maori.

Putaruru

As well as being a service town for the surrounding farming area, Putaruru is also a timber milling centre.

The township was surveyed in 1905, but, like other Waikato towns, did not grow till farming became successful in the 1930s when measures were taken to restore fertility to the cobalt-deficient soils.

Springtime comes in bright colours to the gardens of the Waikato, as a contrast with the greenness which dominates the region year-round. Here, on the streets of Putaruru, rhododendrons, originally from the Himalayan mountains, brighten the scene.

Tirau

Tirau township. This small town plays a pivotal role in the road network of the district; as well as straddling the main national highway (State Highway 1), it has offshoot highways east to Rotorua, and north to Matamata. When first planned it was to be called Oxford but later settlers would have none of that and returned to its original name, Tirau, meaning 'a stake in the ground'. Cambridge, however, stuck to Cambridge.

Just east of Tirau, the road to Rotorua (State Highway 3) twists and turns through some rolling hill country.

Previous pages: Plane trees line a country road near Okoroire Springs, north of Tirau.

Matamata

Above: Matamata sits on the flat Matamata Plain. It is the main servicing centre for a large dairying district which also has several horse stud farms. The name, meaning 'headland', was also the name of a pa near here, built on a promontory projecting out into the surrounding swamp. The name also implies a special place of vision or prophecy.

Opposite: Seen from above, a horse stud farm presents an image of beautiful landscaping using trees and hedges.

Country Art

Sometimes selling something.
Sometimes just something done to express the creative mood of the artist.

Above: The wealth of the Waikato rests on four teats and an udder. Robert Hewitt, like hundreds of other dairy farmers throughout the district, has a very early start to the day.

Previous pages: These rich productive pastures are the basis of the dairy industry. A third of New Zealand's export earnings are from these lands. Once forest and swamp, they now grow grasses year round.

The early morning sun is just breaking through the night-time fog as the cows leave the milking-shed. The cycle continues: back to the fields to eat more grass before the next milking, later this afternoon. If you stop anywhere on the Waikato plains in the early hours, before sunrise and when the air is still, the chances are you will hear the sounds of a milking shed: the rhythmical pumping of the mechanical milking machine, the sounds of music from the radio found in every shed, and the low, gentle complaints of the cows.

Top left: The Waitoa Dairy factory near Morrinsville; one of the new "super-factories."

Below: Milk tankers are the most common vehicles on Waikato back-roads in the early morning, as they collect milk from the myriad farm milking sheds scattered throughout the region. They reminded me of bees on their mission to gather nectar to take back to the hive. Where there were once about 150 small dairy factories scattered throughout the Waikato, now economies of scale have resulted in just a handful of large "super-factories". In this way, from grasses to udders to exports, the Waikato has become one huge production system.

Morrinsville

Morrinsville

Te Aroha

Horotiu

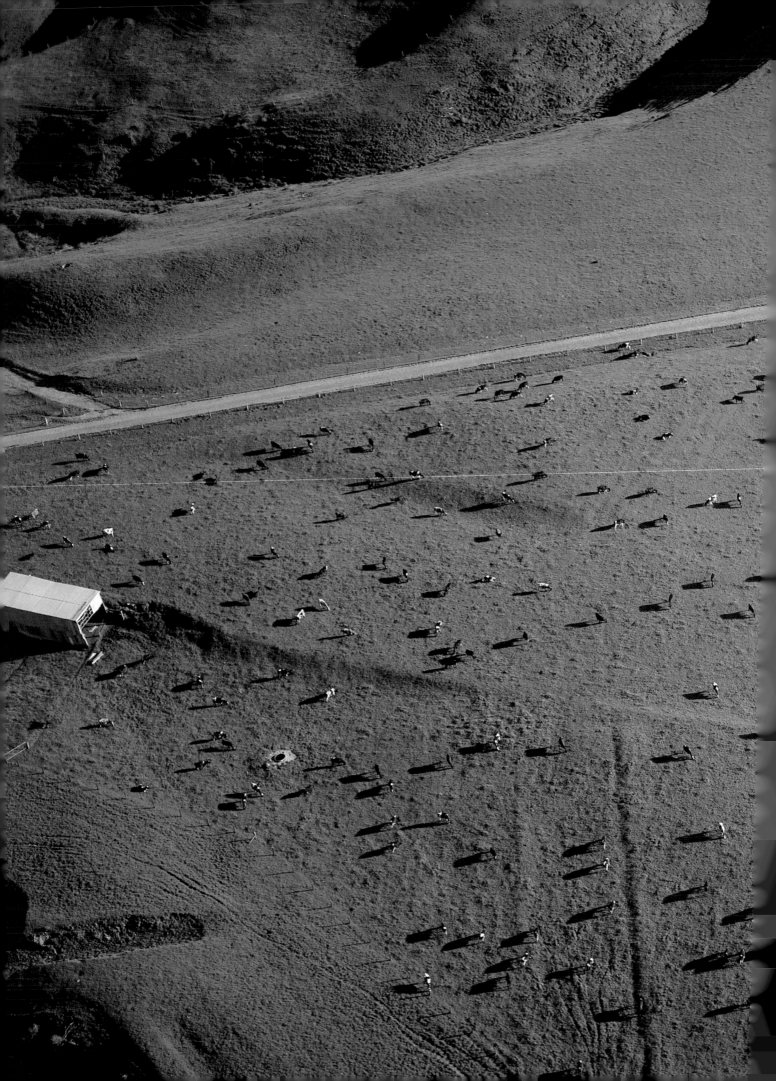

Morrinsville

Above: Morrinsville, the township at the hub of New Zealand's most intensively farmed dairying district.
Before European settlement the land was lowlying water-logged swampland.
It was crossed by an old Maori route between the Waihou basin and the Ngaruawahia area on the Waikato River.
European settlement dates from 1874 when the brothers Thomas and Samuel Morrin purchased 12,000 hectares from the Maori owners and established a settlement for their farm workers.
The railway link with Hamilton in the early 1880s brought an increase in land value and made swamp drainage an economic proposition.

Previous pages: The dairy wealth of the Waikato rests upon some of the most suitable soils and climates found anywhere, on the scientific pasture management techniques developed by the world renowned Ruakura Research Station, and on the sheer skill of Waikato farmers.
Herds of 200 plus, like the one seen in this aerial view, are not uncommon.

Green and lush hill country between Morrinsville and Cambridge.

Above: The Kaimai Range forms a barrier to the eastern edge of the Waikato Plains. This rugged and heavily forested mountain range rises to a height of 950 metres at its highest point, Mt Te Aroha. It contains the Kaimai-Mamaku Forest Park and a covering of native forest comprises kauri, rimu, tawa, miro, matai, totara and the most northerly stands of silver and red beech.
Possum, deer, and goats have severely damaged the original cover, but the eroded slopes seen here are as much the consequence of steepness, heavy rainfall, and soils too thin to hold the vegetation. Conservation strategies to protect the forests are in place.

Opposite: A 30-minute walk through native bush brings you to the spectacular Wairere Falls, plunging 153 metres over a rocky escarpment. The track zig-zags up the steep mountainside to the right of the falls. This track was once the most important Maori trail crossing the Kaimai range, providing access to Tauranga Harbour in the east.

An overnight car crash has left this poor goat puzzled. Chained inside its shelter, it must have received quite a shock in the darkness of the night. Only the fortunate placement of a concrete powerpole has saved it from a worse fate.

Objets d' Art

Port Waikato

near Shaftesbury

Pukerewa Road

Hamilton

near Mangaiti

Te Aroha

Te Aroha

Above: Te Aroha township was an early point of settlement and contact, and a gateway to the plains of Hauraki. Situated on the eastern perimeter of the Waikato, it is nestled against the lower slopes of the Kaimai Range. The town gained its name from the great love which the navigator, a priest of the Tainui, bore for his wife.

The first European settler on the site of the future town was Charles Lipsey who came over from the Thames goldfields in 1875 and built the first weatherboard house. For a time the township was known as Lipseytown. The Waihou river was dredged in 1880 and Te Aroha became a riverport with a direct link to Auckland. Plans for it to become the commercial hub of the Waikato never eventuated, however.

Previous pages: Those who live in and love the Waikato will tell you one secret of that love: in the early mornings and in the evenings, the greens become golden and the landscape comes alive.

The Waihou River drains the Kaimai Range and weaves a sinuous path northward to the Thames estuary through an old river plain of the Waikato River.

Ox-bow lakes abound here. These were once riverbed but have been deserted by the river to be left as small lakes.

In 1769 Captain Cook looked at these flatlands, then covered with dense kahikatea forest, and imagined that one day a great city might rise here, a London of the south perhaps. But these were really wetlands till grid-like drainage made pasture possible.

Above: The old Bathhouse at Te Aroha.
Known locally as the Cadman Building, it was built in 1898. It originally housed 19 tepid and hotwater mineral bathtubs, each in a separate cubicle.
Te Aroha was famous for its mineral springs, bringing visitors from far and wide; 30,000 would come in a year. The bathhouse closed in 1962, when many of the tubs were bought by local farmers for water troughs for their stock.
The buiiding now contains a local museum, while modern spa pools have been built behind.

Opposite: The Great War statue, Te Aroha.
Every New Zealand town has a war memorial. Te Aroha has two; this one for World War I and a clock tower just down the street for World War II.
Carved in Canadian granite by an Italian sculptor, it represents a New Zealand infantryman.

Rural Delivery

Mailman, Bob Jeffries.

Above: A man and his family. Left to right: Peg-Sue, Sam, Ginge, Muffin and Barry.

Opposite: Pets' day at Netherton Primary School.

Ngaruawahia

Ngaruawahia, 'the two places made one'.
The uniting place of the two great rivers of the region, the Waikato and the Waipa. Today it symbolises the unity of Maori and Pakeha.
Ngaruawahia has significance as the capital of the Waikato Maori people. Their paramount marae is here at Turangawaewae. This is the ceremonial centre for the Maori queen, Dame Te Atairangikaahu, and is a national meeting place for all tribes, government and official visitors, royal guests from many places, and, at all such times, just ordinary folk.

The bronze bust of Princess Te Puea gazes proudly over the marae she created from wasteland at Turangawaewae. She was a key figure in the Maori King movement when the headquarters was re-established at Ngaruawahia in 1921, and played a leading role in the Maori renaissance of this century.

With only a limited amount of formal education she became a passionate student of the Bible and of tribal lore, and a dominating force behind the self-help development of the Maori.

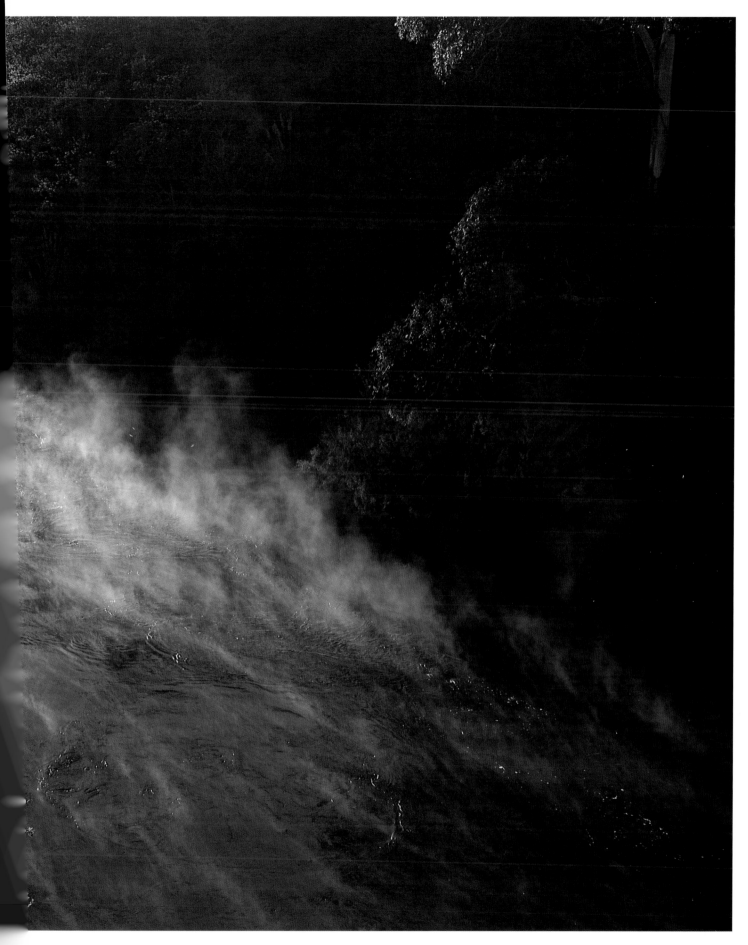

Waikato taniwha rau
He piko he taniwha   Waikato of a thousand water spirits
He piko he taniwha   At every bend another

Huntly

Above: Dominated by the huge coal and gas-fired power station, the township of Huntly occupies a long narrow strip along both banks of the Waikato River.

Opposite: The large open-cast coalmine, Rotowaro, near Glen Afton supplies local coal to the nearby power station at Huntly.
This is the largest mine of the Waikato coalfield. The coalmining industry was first established here on a commercial basis in 1876.

Duckhunters' mai-mais dot the broad shallow waters of Lake Waikare.
This is the largest lake in the Waikato, one of many in the north-west part of the region, known as the Lower Waikato River Basin. Lakes such as this provide important water storage areas to lessen the effects of flooding when the Waikato River is high.
The Whangamarino Wetland near here is an internationally recognised wetland and an important home for wildfowl and many threatened species of wildlife.

Cabbage trees define a pocket of wetland near the rivermouth.
Only 5 percent of the original wetlands of the Waikato have escaped development into pasture.
There are two main areas where these remain: the Lower Waikato Basin, (north of Huntly), and the Hamilton Basin between Ngaruawahia and Te Awamutu.
The wetlands of Waikato were a 'treasure trove' for Maori. They were a valuable source of food including eel, birds and fish, and provided other products such as feathers and flax for weaving and rope-making.

He Taonga Nga Repo Me Nga Roto
The swamplands and lakes are treasures